A NOTE TO PARENTS

Learning to read is an exciting time in your child's life! This book will help aspiring readers get started on their journeys.

All-Star Readers were created to help make learning to read a fun and engaging experience. Carefully selected stories and subject matter support the acquisition of reading skills, encourage children to learn about the world around them, and help develop a life-long love of books.

This Discovery Level 1 and Level 2 collection offers fascinating factual content that is carefully crafted for new and developing readers. Every child is unique, and age or grade level does not determine a particular reading level. See the previous page for descriptions of the reading levels in this book.

As you read with your child, read for short periods of time and pause often. Encourage them to sound out words they do not know. Suggest they look at the picture on the page for clues about what the word might be. Have younger children turn the pages and point to pictures and familiar words. Each story in this book includes a glossary that defines new vocabulary words. When your child comes across a boldfaced word they don't recognize, instruct them to turn to the glossary and read its definition.

A good way to reinforce reading comprehension is to have a conversation about the book after finishing it. Children love talking about their favorite parts! As your child becomes a more independent reader, encourage them to discuss ideas and questions they may have.

Remember that there is no right or wrong way to share books with your child. When you find time to read with your child, you create a pattern of enjoying and exploring books that will become a love of reading!

CONTENTS

Discovery™

I Am a
TIGER

Level 1

Written by Lori C. Froeb

Silver Dolphin

Raaar! I am a tiger cub.

I am small now.

One day I will be a big cat.

Tigers are the biggest
cats on Earth!

There are six kinds of tigers alive today.

All tigers live in Asia.

Asia is a large **continent**.

Bengal tiger

Malayan tiger

Can you tell us apart?

ASIA

South
China tiger

Siberian tiger

Sumatran tiger

Indochinese
tiger

I am a Siberian tiger.

My family lives in a country called Russia.

Siberia is part of Russia.

We live in the forest.
It can get very cold in winter!

RUSSIA

I live here!

The world has many big cats.

cheetah

jaguar

tiger

lion

leopard

Siberian tigers are the biggest cats of all.

I will be six hundred pounds one day.

My body will be ten feet long from head to tail!

All tigers have striped coats.
Our skin is striped too.
The stripes are **camouflage**.

They help us blend in with the grass and trees.

We hide from our **prey**. We sneak closer until it is time to pounce.

Tigers are carnivores.
That means we eat meat.

We eat a lot at once.
We do not always eat
every day.

I am too young to hunt.

My mom hunts for our food.

My sister and I watch her.

We will learn to hunt from her.

Most of the time mom hunts for wild boar.

They are pigs with long hair.

She also hunts for elk and even bears.

Sometimes large prey is hard to find.

Then mom brings us rabbits or fish!

We cannot wait to hunt on our own.

Tigers are expert hunters.
Our bodies are made for it!

legs

Our back legs are strong.
We can leap thirty feet!

ears

We can **swivel** our ears to hear prey.

eyes

We can see very well in day or night.

teeth

Our teeth can be three inches long. They grip and tear prey.

feet

Our padded feet are very quiet. This makes it easy to surprise prey.

17

Adult tigers do not live in groups.
Adult tigers live and hunt alone.
I will stay with my mother until I am two.

Then I will find a **territory** of my own.

A territory is where a tiger lives and hunts.

Tigers mark their territory.
We scratch trees with our nails.
Other tigers see the scratches.

The scratches mean the
area belongs to another tiger.

Our nails can be four inches long!

They are tucked in when not being used.

They stay very sharp.

We also use urine (pee) to mark things.

Mom is not smiling here! She is sniffing the scent left by another tiger.

She opens her mouth to get a better sniff.

She learns about the other tiger.

She can tell if it is male or female and how old it is.

I try to sniff too!

Most cats do not like the water.
Tigers are not like most cats.
We like the water!

We play in the water and take baths.

Tigers are also great swimmers.

Some have swum miles to cross rivers.

We also use sound to talk to each other.

A tiger's roar can be heard two miles away!

We can also growl and hiss. We cannot purr like house cats.

Not all tigers are orange.

Some tigers are white.

All white tigers are Bengal tigers.

White tigers have blue eyes.
About one white tiger is born out of ten thousand cubs.

There are about two hundred white tigers on Earth.

There used to be many tigers in the wild.

Now there are fewer than four thousand left.

Our **habitats** are shrinking.

Humans hunt us.

We are **endangered**. This means we may one day disappear.

If humans protect us, we will survive.

We will rule the jungle once again!

Glossary

camouflage: an animal's coloring that helps it hide and blend in

continent: one of seven large pieces of land on Earth

endangered: almost none left in the world

habitats: places where animals live

prey: an animal that is hunted by other animals for food

swivel: to move in different directions

territory: the area where an animal lives and hunts

Discovery™

I Am a
PENGUIN

Level 1

Written by Lori C. Froeb

Silver Dolphin

Hi there! I am a penguin.
This is my family.
We are emperor penguins.

There are eighteen **species** of penguins.

Emperor penguins are the largest species.

I am a male penguin.

I weigh about sixty pounds. That is about the same as an eight-year-old human.

I am about four feet tall.

We live where it is very cold.

It is a place called Antarctica.

Antarctica is on the South Pole.

Galápagos penguin

equator

Magellanic penguin

chinstrap penguin

Most penguin species live south of the **equator**.

Only the Galápagos penguin lives north of the equator.

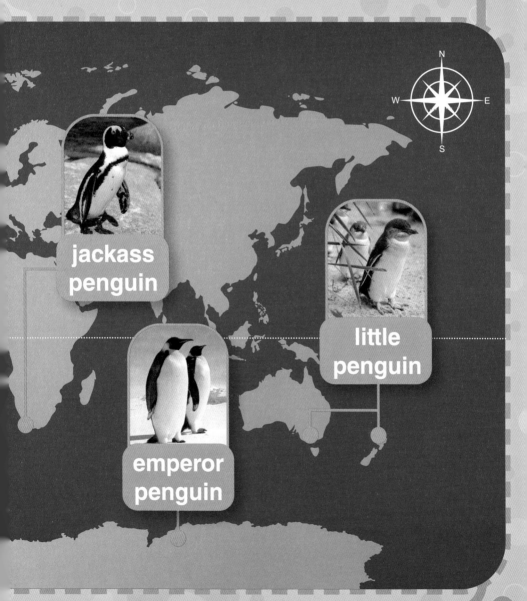

jackass penguin

little penguin

emperor penguin

Not all penguins live in cold places.

This penguin lives in Africa.

It is called a jackass penguin.

It makes a sound like a donkey.

The smallest penguin lives in Australia.

It is called a little penguin.

Little penguins are only a foot tall.

They are blue and white.

Penguins are birds, but we cannot fly.

Half of our time is spent in the water.

We use our wings as flippers to swim.

Small penguins stay near the surface.

Large penguins like me can dive deep.

I can hold my breath for twenty-two minutes!

Penguins are **carnivores**. We hunt small animals in the ocean.

squid

krill

My favorite food is fish. I also eat squid and tiny animals called krill.

Penguins do not chew their food.

Our mouths are spiny and rough inside.

Slippery fish cannot get away.

We swallow our food whole.

We are quick in the water.

But we are slower on land.

We have short legs and waddle as we walk.

We can move quicker if we hop.

Sometimes we slide on our bellies.

We use our feet to push us forward.

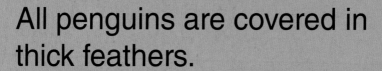

All penguins are covered in thick feathers.

Our feathers are very close together.

They trap air near our skin.

This keeps us warm in the water and on land.

Feathers wear out.
Penguins **molt** at least once a year.

During a molt, all of a penguin's feathers fall out.
New feathers replace the old ones.

My mate and I live in a **colony**.

A colony is a group of penguins.

Our colony sometimes has one thousand birds.

We all nest and hunt together.

This year my mate and
I had a chick.

It was hard work!

I met my mate in April.

April is the beginning of winter in Antarctica.

It is a very cold time to lay an egg.

There is ice on the ground.

My mate laid her egg in May.
She carefully placed the egg
on my feet.

The egg could not touch the ice.
The chick inside would freeze.

I balanced the egg on my feet. I tucked it under my tummy pouch. The egg was safe and warm there.

Then my mate left to hunt for food.

I did not see her for two months.

But I was not alone.

All the dads in my colony stuck together.

We huddled to stay warm in the wind.

We took turns being on the cold outside.

I protected the egg for sixty-four days.

I did not eat.

I made sure my egg stayed warm.

Then one day the egg hatched!

The chick still had to be kept warm. She stayed on my feet under my pouch.

I fed the chick a liquid from my throat.

Finally, the mother penguins returned.

Some walked fifty miles or more back to the colony.

My mate called to me and I answered.

I was so happy to see her!

Then it was my turn to look for food.

While I was gone, my mate fed the chick.

She **regurgitated** food from her stomach.

The chick was always hungry!

We took turns caring for
the chick.

She grew fast!

Now our chick huddles with her friends while we hunt.

This group of young penguins is called a **creche**.

I hear my chick calling.
It is my turn to feed her.
Thank you for visiting!

Glossary

carnivores: animals that eat meat

colony: a group of animals living together

creche: a group of young animals that stay together for warmth

equator: an imaginary line around Earth that is halfway between the North and South Poles

molt: when feathers fall out to make room for new ones

regurgitated: brought food up out of the stomach

species: a group of living things different from all other groups

Discovery

I Am a
DOLPHIN

Level 1

Written by Lori C. Froeb

Silver Dolphin

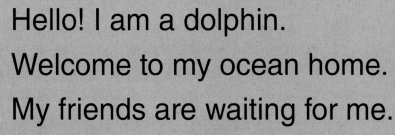

Hello! I am a dolphin.
Welcome to my ocean home.
My friends are waiting for me.

Come on! You can meet them.

I live in a group of dolphins called a **pod**.

The pod plays, hunts, and swims together.

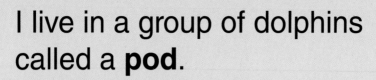

We talk to each other with clicks and whistles.

We each have our own whistle.

My whistle is how others know me.

It is like having a name.

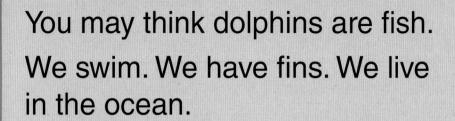

You may think dolphins are fish. We swim. We have fins. We live in the ocean.

But we are not fish.
We are **mammals**,
just like you.

We are **warm-blooded**. We breathe air.

We drink milk from our mothers when we are babies.

Dolphins are related to whales and porpoises.

humpback whale

beluga whale

porpoise

We are also related to hippos.
It is true!
The hippo is our closest living **relative**.

I am a bottlenose dolphin.
My body is all gray.

I live in the warmer parts of
the ocean.

There are thirty-nine other **species** of dolphin.

Most live in the ocean.

Some live in rivers.

Atlantic spotted dolphin

dusky dolphin

short-beaked common dolphin

spinner dolphin

Not all dolphins are gray.

The Amazon river dolphin
is pink!

She has a long thin snout.

Orcas are called killer whales.

But orcas are not whales.

Orcas are dolphins!

They are the largest dolphins in the world.

Do you see the hole in my head?

That is my blowhole.

All dolphins have one.

I must come to the water's surface to breathe.

I breathe through my blowhole.

I can also use it to make sound.

I use my blowhole to make my whistles and clicks!

I am getting hungry.
My pod is ready to hunt for food.

Big dolphins like orcas hunt for seals.

Some orcas even hunt sharks.

Bottlenose dolphins like to eat small fish and squid.

I hear some fish nearby.

I use sound waves to look for prey.
This is called **echolocation**.

I send a sound into the water.
The sound bounces off objects and back to me.

The sound tells me about the object.
There is a school of fish nearby!

Dolphin pods hunt fish together.
They herd the fish into a large ball.

Then each dolphin swims through the ball.

We catch fish as we swim through.

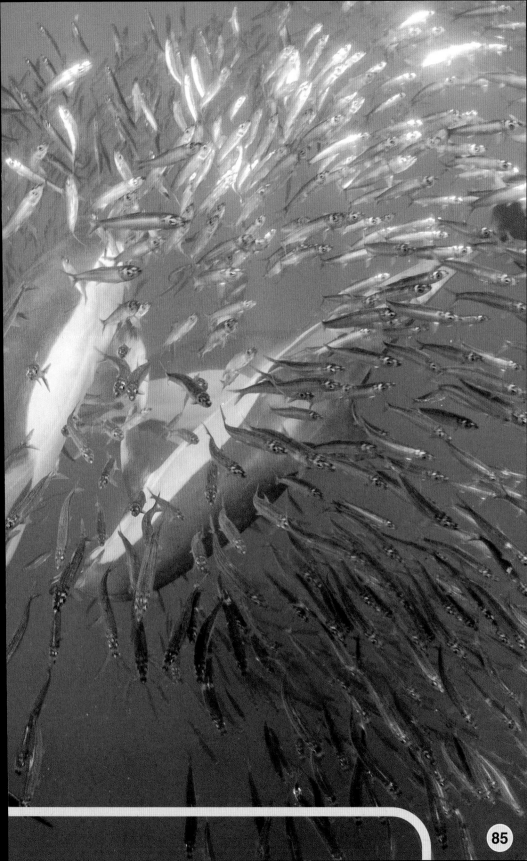

Some dolphins hunt another way.

They make a ring of mud in the water.

The fish jump out of the water to escape the mud.

The dolphins catch jumping fish!

Dolphins do not chew their food.
Our teeth are only good for grabbing.
We swallow our food whole.

After lunch, it is time to play.

We love to play!

It is fun to flip out of the water.

We also like to surf the waves.

Sometimes we play catch.

We use things like seaweed, sponges, or coral.

Some of us make bubble rings for fun.

Jumping out of the water is fun. It also makes it easier to get around.

Swimming in water takes a lot of energy.

Moving through air is much easier.

This is why dolphins jump out of the water while swimming.

It is called **porpoising**.

Dolphins are curious and smart.
Some of us like to be around humans.

We sometimes play and swim together with humans.

Some dolphins have saved humans from drowning.

Some dolphins work with humans.

The dolphins are trained to look for lost swimmers.

The dolphins are rewarded with fish.

I hope you liked meeting my pod.
We are going to look for some waves.

It is surf time!

Glossary

echolocation: a method dolphins use to find objects using sound waves

mammals: animals that are warm-blooded and feed milk to their babies

pod: a group of dolphins, porpoises, or whales

porpoising: to jump out of the water while swimming

relative: someone who came from the same ancestor

species: a group of living things different from all other groups

warm-blooded: able to control one's body temperature

Discovery

I Am a
SHARK

Level 2

Written by Lori C. Froeb

Silver Dolphin

I am a shark. There are over four hundred species of sharks on Earth.

I am a great white shark. I am the largest **predator** in the ocean!

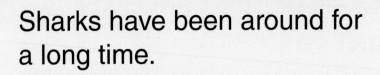

Sharks have been around for a long time.

We have been around for more than four hundred million years!

My biggest **ancestor** was megalodon.

Scientists believe megalodon grew up to sixty feet long.

That's longer than a school bus!

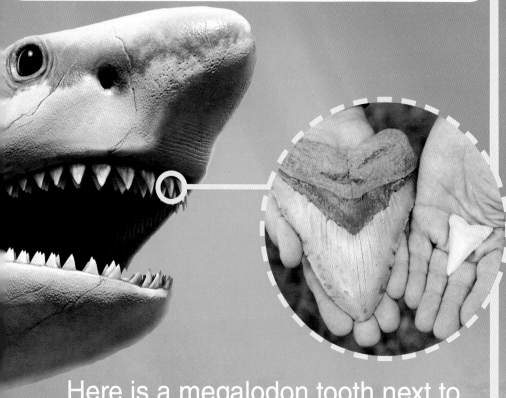

Here is a megalodon tooth next to one of my teeth.

Many scientists believe megalodon was the largest fish to ever live.

Great white sharks are probably the most famous sharks.

We have even been in many movies!

But sharks come in many shapes and sizes.

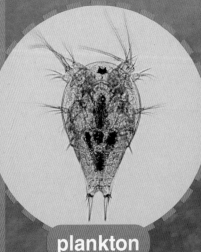

plankton

This is a whale shark. She is the biggest fish in the world!

She may be big, but she eats tiny creatures called **plankton**.

This is a hammerhead.

His head shape lets him see **prey** better than other sharks.

He also uses his head to catch food. He pins down prey in the sand, then eats it.

This is a zebra shark.

She has spots now, but when she was born she had stripes like a zebra.

The zebra shark spends most of her time on the ocean floor.

This is a thresher shark.
Check out that long tail.

The thresher uses his
tail to stun fish by
slapping them.

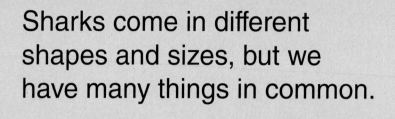

Sharks come in different shapes and sizes, but we have many things in common.

All sharks are fish. All sharks are cold-blooded.

Our bodies are the same temperature as the water around us.

Sharks don't have bones. Instead, our skeletons are made out of **cartilage**.

Cartilage is flexible and light.

It makes it easier to swim faster and longer.

Every shark has these basic parts:

nose
Sharks have an amazing sense of smell.

eyes
Sharks have eyes, but no eyelids.

gill slits
Sharks can have five, six, or seven gill slits on each side.

jaws
The jaws can move forward to grab prey. Most animal jaws only move up and down.

pectoral fins
These fins help the shark move up and down.

dorsal fins

These fins keep the shark from rolling over.

caudal fin

This tail fin moves back and forth to make the shark move forward.

pelvic fins

These fins help the shark steer and stop.

We have scales like other fish.

Our scales are called **dermal denticles**. Denticle means "little tooth."

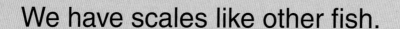

The denticles make shark skin feel like sandpaper.

They make water move over our bodies faster.

To pick up speed, we use our tail fins.

Every species of shark has a different-shaped tail fin.

We move our tail fins back and forth to go forward.

great white shark

blacktip reef shark

hammerhead shark

thresher shark

All sharks have sharp teeth—lots of them!

This is a good thing, because our teeth fall out often.

tiger shark

great white shark

bull shark

mako shark

oceanic whitetip shark

When one tooth falls out, another moves into its place.

A great white can have three hundred teeth in its jaws at one time.

During my lifetime, I may go through thirty thousand teeth.

Adult humans only have thirty-two teeth. If one falls out, it is not replaced.

Most sharks are born alive, but some hatch from egg cases.

A cat shark laid these egg cases.

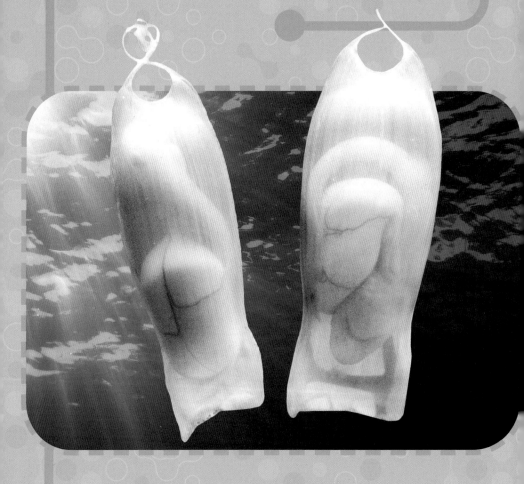

Baby sharks are called pups.

You can see the pups growing inside.

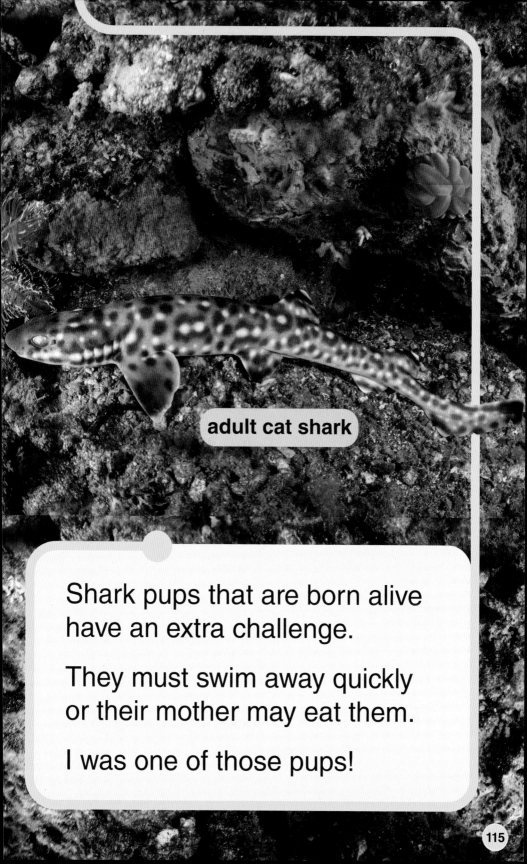

adult cat shark

Shark pups that are born alive have an extra challenge.

They must swim away quickly or their mother may eat them.

I was one of those pups!

Great whites like me like to hang out in the shallow parts of the oceans all around the world.

We like the warmer water that is found there.

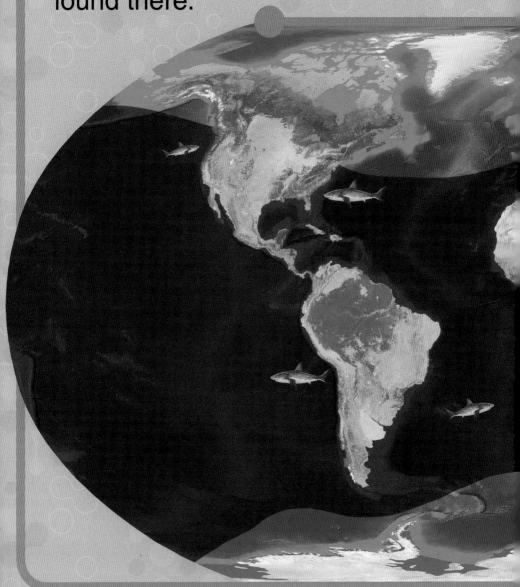

But we also travel to deeper water and farther out to sea.

Usually, I follow my nose to where the food is!

Sharks have an amazing sense of smell.

We can sniff tiny amounts of blood in the water to find prey.

My nose will even tell me which direction the scent is coming from.

Take a close look at my nose.

See those small dots?

They are organs that can feel electrical fields in the water.

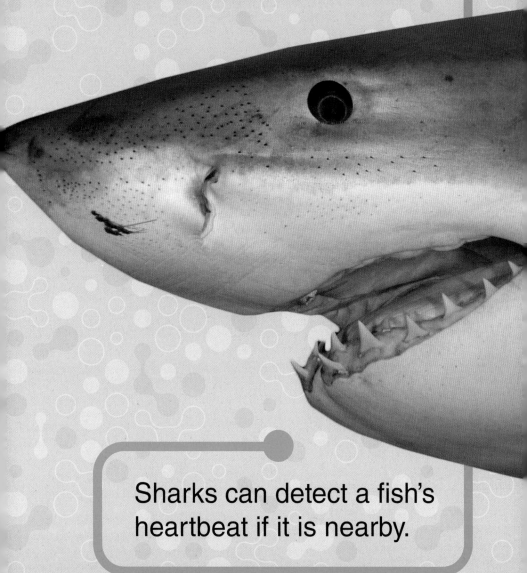

Sharks can detect a fish's heartbeat if it is nearby.

Like all sharks, I am a **carnivore**. This means I eat meat.

Here are some of my favorite foods:

dolphins

sea lions

sea turtles

tuna

rays

Sometimes other sharks!

We do not hunt humans for food.

Sometimes we attack a human by mistake.

Our only predators are humans.

They kill more than one hundred million of us a year.

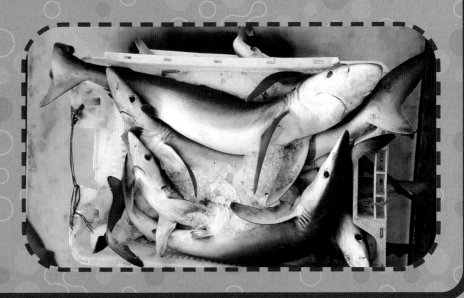

When I hunt, I usually stay above or below my prey.

My belly is white and my back is dark gray.

I am hard to see in the deep water from above.

I am also hard to see in the sunlit water from below.

This is called **countershading**.

I can surprise my prey
because it doesn't see me.

I can surprise my prey another way.

I **breach** to hunt seals near the surface.

To breach, I swim up fast from below the seal.

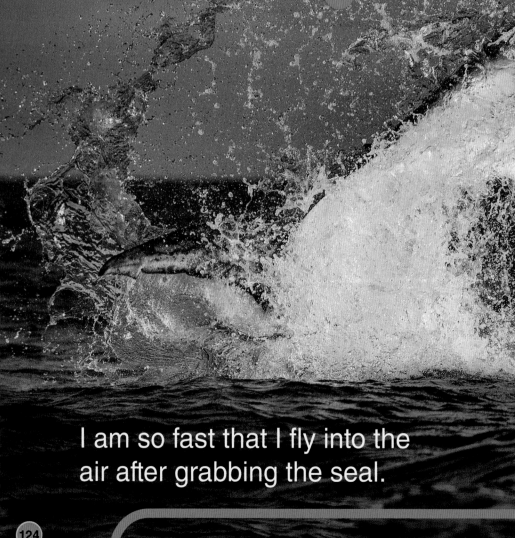

I am so fast that I fly into the air after grabbing the seal.

I splash back into the water and enjoy my meal.

Great whites are one of the few shark species that do this.

All this talk about hunting has made me hungry!

I am going to go grab something to eat.

See you later!

Super Shark Stats!

Fastest

The mako shark can swim sixty miles per hour. That is as fast as a car on the highway!

Toothiest

A bull shark can have three hundred fifty teeth in its mouth at one time.

Biggest

The whale shark can weigh as much as four elephants.

Hardest to Spot

The wobbegong shark uses **camouflage** to blend in with the seafloor. Can you find it?

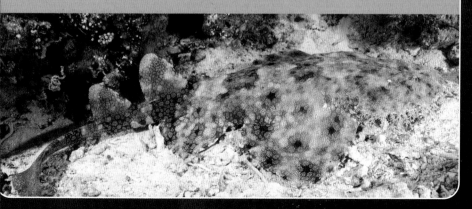

Glossary

ancestor: a creature that lived in the past, a relative

breach: to swim upward fast enough to leave the water

camouflage: an animal's coloring that helps it hide and blend in

carnivore: an animal that eats meat

cartilage: a light, rubbery material from which a shark's skeleton is made

countershading: a type of camouflage where the bottom of the body is light and the top is dark

dermal denticles: tiny toothlike scales covering a shark's skin

plankton: tiny animals that float near the ocean's surface

predator: an animal that hunts other animals for food

prey: an animal that is hunted by other animals for food

Discovery

I Am a
GORILLA

Level 2

Written by Lori C. Froeb

Silver Dolphin

Hello! Welcome to Africa.

I am a gorilla.

There are two **species** of gorillas.

Western gorillas live in rain forests and marshes in western Africa.

They live in Cameroon, Gabon, and a few other countries.

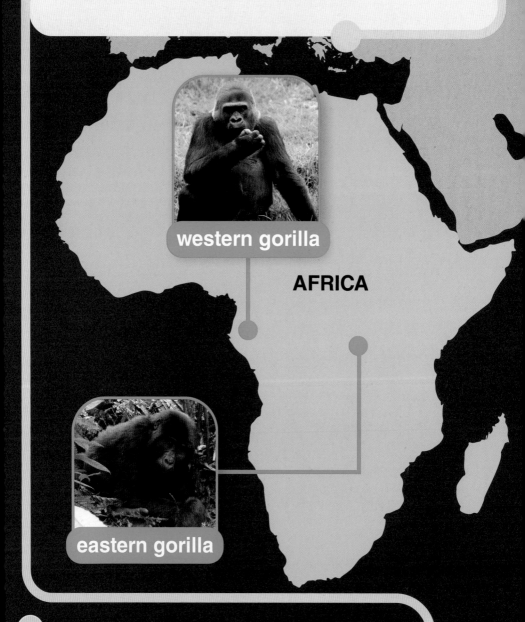

western gorilla

AFRICA

eastern gorilla

Eastern gorillas live in mountain forests in parts of central Africa.

They are found in Rwanda, Uganda, and the Congo.

I am an eastern gorilla.

Gorillas are great apes.

Bonobos, orangutans, and chimpanzees are also great apes.

Apes do not have tails like monkeys do.

gorilla
largest of the apes

bonobo
most peaceful of the apes

Monkey, not an ape!

Monkeys have tails. Apes do not.

orangutan

spends most of its life in trees

chimpanzee

closest **relative** to humans

Most apes live in Africa just like me!

Orangutans live in Asia.

135

Look at me. Do you think you and I look a little alike?

Humans, gorillas, and all apes are **primates**.

Monkeys are primates too.

Primates have big brains and eyes that face forward.

Primates also have long fingers and toes.

Most primates have **opposable thumbs**.

This means we can use our thumbs to grasp things.

Humans and gorillas share more than ninety-six percent of their DNA.

DNA is what makes us what we are. It is in all our cells.

No wonder we look a little alike!

You are part of a family. I am part of a family too.

My mom and I are part of a **troop**. A troop is a group of gorillas.

We do everything together.

My dad is in charge of the troop. He is a silverback.

The hair on his back turned silver when he became a teenager.

When I get older, I will be a silverback too.

Dad makes sure our troop is safe.

He decides where we look for food.

If there is a fight in the troop, Dad breaks it up.

Gorillas are peaceful apes.

Most times there are no fights.

But Dad is always on the lookout for trouble.

If he sees a male gorilla he does not know, he may roar.

Sometimes he will beat his chest.

The other gorilla knows this means, "I am in charge."

Gorillas do not have many predators.

But our numbers in the wild are shrinking.

Humans are the biggest danger to gorillas.

Humans hunt and capture gorillas.

They also destroy gorilla **habitats**.

Today, all gorillas are **endangered**.

Gorillas use twenty-five sounds to **communicate**.

We can scream if we are angry or scared.

We hum when we eat.

A hum means we are happy.

A mother gorilla can make a grunting sound like a pig.

She uses this to tell her baby he is doing something wrong.

All gorillas walk using their knuckles and legs.

This would be very hard for you to do.

It is easy for us.

Our arms are very strong and much longer than our legs.

We can stand and walk on our feet too.

This is helpful when we are carrying food.

Speaking of food, it is time to look for some with my troop.

Eastern gorillas are **herbivores**.

We **forage** for many hours every day.

We spend all morning looking for food. Then we nap.

When we wake up, we forage for the rest of the day.

Western gorillas are also mainly herbivores.

Fruit is easy to find in their forest, so they eat a lot of it.

They eat more than one hundred different kinds of fruit!

If fruit is hard to find, these gorillas eat leaves and bark.

Some also like to eat ants and termites.

ant

bark

leaves

termite

A hungry western gorilla may look for a termite nest.

He breaks the nest to get at the juicy termites inside.

All this foraging and eating has made me sleepy.

My troop gets ready to nap by building nests.

Mom finds branches and leaves.

She makes a nest for us on the ground.

We make a new nest every time we sleep.

I am learning how to make a nest from my mom.

After naptime, I like to play with my friends.

We climb trees, swing from branches, and wrestle.

Sometimes we even play tag!

Gorillas learn from playing.

We learn how to get along with others in our group.

We also learn how to use our arms to swing.

My friends are calling me to play right now.

See you later!

Gorillas Are Great!

An adult gorilla can eat sixty pounds of food a day!

A baby gorilla can ride on its mother's back when it is four months old. It holds on tightly.

A gorilla noseprint is like a human fingerprint. No two are exactly alike!

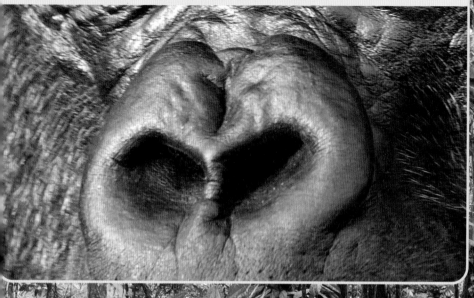

Gorillas get the water they need from plants they eat.

Glossary

communicate: to share information, ideas, and feelings

endangered: almost none left in the world

forage: to look around for food

habitats: places where animals live

herbivores: animals that eat only plants

opposable thumbs: thumbs that can be used to grasp and hold things

primates: a type of mammal that has hands that can grasp, forward-facing eyes, and large brains for their size

relative: someone who came from the same ancestor

species: a group of living things different from all other groups

troop: a group of gorillas

Discovery

I Am a POLAR BEAR

Level 2

Written by Lori C. Froeb

Silver Dolphin

Hi there! Welcome to my chilly home.

I am a polar bear and these are my cubs.

We do not see humans very often.

We live far from any cities or towns.

All polar bears live in the Arctic.

The Arctic is the northernmost part of Earth.

Winters are long, dark, and cold in the Arctic.

Summers are short and cool.

Polar bears live in Russia, Norway, Greenland, Canada, and Alaska in the United States.

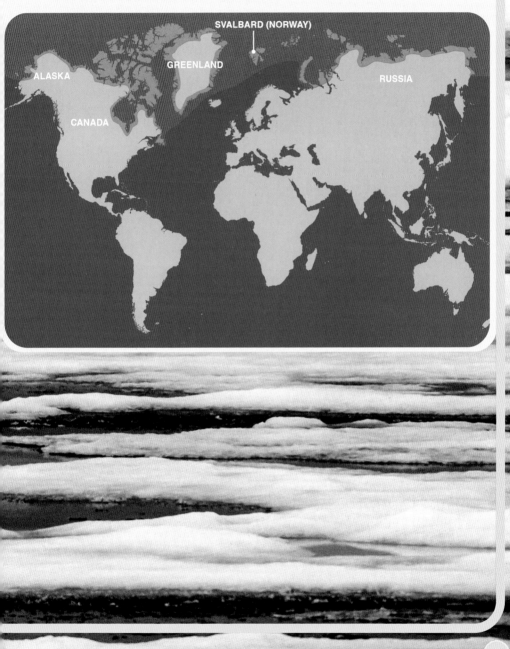

The Arctic is covered by snow and ice for most of the year.

The temperature can drop to minus fifty degrees in winter.

But I am not cold.

Polar bears are covered with very thick fur.

My fur looks white, but each strand is clear.

My fur is very warm and good **camouflage**.

I am hard to spot if I am lying still in the snow.

Under all this fur, my skin is black.

The black color absorbs the sun's light and warms me up!

My body has another way of staying warm: **blubber**!

Blubber is fat. I have a layer of blubber under my skin.

It is four inches thick in places.

The blubber keeps me warm when I swim in the icy water.

Polar bears are great at swimming!

We can swim for days if we need to.

Look at my front paws. They are as big as dinner plates.

I use my front paws like giant paddles in the water.

My paws are great for walking on the snow and ice too.

The bottoms are covered in tiny bumps.

The bumps grip the slippery ice.

Polar bears are **marine mammals**.

The ocean provides us with food and a place to live.

sea otter

polar bear

dolphin

bearded seal

Dolphins, sea otters, and seals are also marine mammals.

Seals are our favorite food!

Polar bears are the largest **predators** with four legs.

Male bears can weigh as much as ten adult humans.

Females like me are much smaller.

Polar bears spend most of their lives floating on **sea ice**.

Sea ice is frozen ocean water.

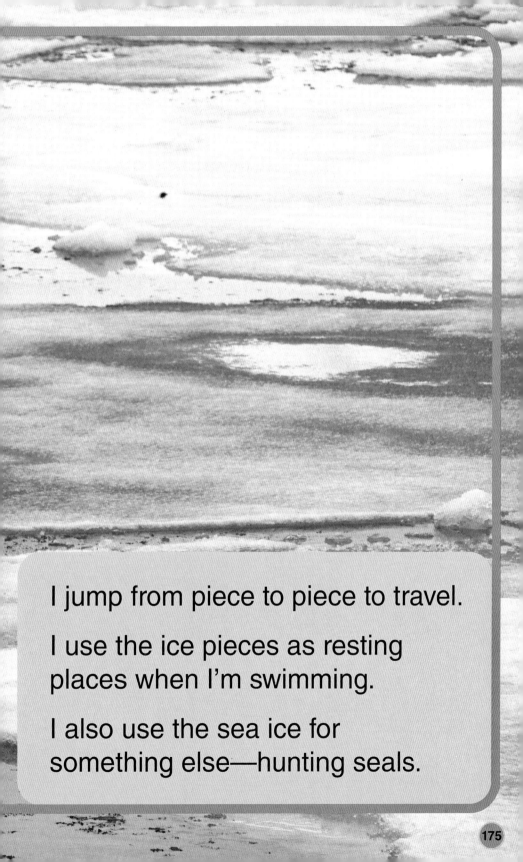

I jump from piece to piece to travel.

I use the ice pieces as resting places when I'm swimming.

I also use the sea ice for something else—hunting seals.

Seals come to holes in the ice to breathe.

I can smell a seal's breathing hole from a mile away.

I follow my nose to the hole.

Then I wait quietly and watch the hole.

When a seal pops out of the hole to breathe, I quickly grab it.

My cubs learn how to hunt from watching me.

The sea ice is around from fall to spring.

We eat as many seals as we can.

The seals' blubber makes us fat.

When the sea ice melts in the summer, we move to shore.

There is not much to eat until the ice returns in the fall.

Sometimes a whale **carcass** washes up on the beach.

We eat its blubber and share with other polar bears.

This carcass was a lucky find.

Sometimes a hungry polar bear may hunt a musk ox or reindeer.

Some polar bears will eat seaweed or birds.

None of these things are as good for us as seals.

Many of us eat nothing for months.

We live off our fat until fall.

Earth is warming up and it is taking longer for sea ice to form.

We are spending more time on land.

It is getting harder to find food.

For this reason, polar bears are **vulnerable**.

This means our numbers are getting smaller.

If we do not find a way to survive, we will be **endangered**.

My cubs are strong.

I take good care of them.

I ate a lot of food in the spring before they were born.

I gained more than four hundred pounds!

In the fall, I dug a den in the snow.

I went into the den and rested.

Polar bears don't **hibernate** like other bears.

I did not move much and did not eat for seven months.

Polar bears usually have one, two, or three cubs.

I had two. Twins!

They were born in winter with their eyes closed.

They each weighed less than two pounds.

That is about as much as a small rabbit.

They drank my milk and grew quickly.

In the spring, we left the den.

The cubs learned to walk, swim, and play.

I finally got something to eat.

It has been seven months since my last meal!

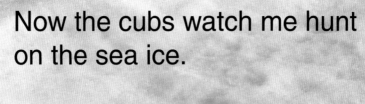

Now the cubs watch me hunt on the sea ice.

I smell a seal nearby. It is time for the cubs' lesson.

See you later!

Polar Bear Fact File

Polar bears roll in the snow to clean themselves. Clean fur is warmer than dirty fur.

Polar bears are more likely to be too hot than too cold. A quick swim cools them down.

Almost sixty percent of polar bears live in Canada. That is about sixteen thousand polar bears.

Polar bears are not hunted by any other animals. Humans are polar bears' only predator.

Glossary

blubber: a layer of fat that marine animals use for warmth and energy

camouflage: an animal's coloring that helps it hide and blend in

carcass: a dead body, usually of an animal

endangered: almost none left in the world

hibernate: to go into a deep sleep for the winter. Animals don't eat or drink while hibernating.

marine mammals: mammals that depend on the ocean to live. Whales, polar bears, and sea otters are marine mammals.

predators: animals that hunt other animals for food

sea ice: frozen ocean water

vulnerable: a species that will become endangered if its habitat keeps shrinking